Quick Guide to Flash Catalyst

Quick Guide to Flash Catalyst

Rafiq Elmansy

O'REILLY®

Beijing · Cambridge · Farnham · Köln · Sebastopol · Tokyo

Quick Guide to Flash Catalyst

by Rafiq Elmansy

Published by O'Reilly Media, Inc., 1005 Gravenstein Highway North, Sebastopol, CA 95472.

O'Reilly books may be purchased for educational, business, or sales promotional use. Online editions are also available for most titles (*http://my.safaribooksonline.com*). For more information, contact our corporate/institutional sales department: (800) 998-9938 or *corporate@oreilly.com*.

Editor: Mary Treseler
Production Editor: O'Reilly Publishing Services

Cover Designer: Karen Montgomery
Interior Designer: David Futato
Illustrator: O'Reilly Publishing Services

Printing History:

August 2011:	First Edition.

ISBN: 978-1-449-30674-8

[LSI]

1312551460

This book is dedicated to my parents, who discovered my love of art and design; my beloved wife, who supported me in every step of my life; and my two beautiful daughters.

Table of Contents

Preface vii

1. Introduction to Flash Catalyst 5.5 1

2. Flash Catalyst Components 5
   Button   6
   Checkbox and Radio Button   7
   Horizontal and Vertical Scrollbars   8
   Horizontal and Vertical Sliders   9
   Text Input Component   9
   Toggle Button   10
   Data List Component   11

3. Starting a Flash Catalyst Project 13

4. Interactions and Transitions in Flash Catalyst 33

5. Publishing the Flash Catalyst Project 55
   Project Performance   57

Preface

Conventions Used in This Book

The following typographical conventions are used in this book:

Italic
> Indicates new terms, URLs, email addresses, filenames, file extensions, pathnames, directories, states, events, actions, and menu options.

`Constant width`
> Indicates keyboard accelerators.

> This icon signifies a tip, suggestion, or general note.

> This icon indicates a warning or caution.

Using Code Examples

This book is here to help you get your job done. In general, you may use the code in this book in your programs and documentation. You do not need to contact us for permission unless you're reproducing a significant portion of the code. For example, writing a program that uses several chunks of code from this book does not require permission. Selling or distributing a CD-ROM of examples from O'Reilly books does require permission. Answering a question by citing this book and quoting example code does not require permission. Incorporating a significant amount of example code from this book into your product's documentation does require permission.

We appreciate, but do not require, attribution. An attribution usually includes the title, author, publisher, and ISBN. For example: "*Quick Guide to Flash Catalyst* by Rafiq Elmansy. Copyright 2011 Rafiq Elmansy, 978-1-449-30674-8."

If you feel your use of code examples falls outside fair use or the permission given above, feel free to contact us at *permissions@oreilly.com*.

We'd Like to Hear from You

Please address comments and questions concerning this book to the publisher:

O'Reilly Media, Inc.
1005 Gravenstein Highway North
Sebastopol, CA 95472
(800) 998-9938 (in the United States or Canada)
(707) 829-0515 (international or local)
(707) 829-0104 (fax)

We have a web page for this book, where we list errata, examples, and any additional information. You can access this page at:

http://oreilly.com/catalog/9781449306748/

To comment or ask technical questions about this book, send email to:

bookquestions@oreilly.com

For more information about our books, conferences, Resource Centers, and the O'Reilly Network, see our web site at:

http://www.oreilly.com

Acknowledgments

As a follower of O'Reilly books and news for years, this is a great opportunity for me to have a book published by O'Reilly, thanks to the great efforts of a team who takes care of the book from draft idea to final product.

First of all, I would like to give special thanks to Rich Tretola, who introduced me to this great project and helped me through the book developing process. Also, I would like to thank Mary Treseler for her help during the project and for taking care of it until it reached the final production.

And I would like to thank Karen Shaner, Holly Bauer, and Sarah Schneider for their great support and help with the documentation and SVN server issues. Also, I really appreciate the amazing work of the great team at O'Reilly for their great efforts in the book template design, styling, and other production stages.

CHAPTER 1

Introduction to Flash Catalyst 5.5

Adobe Flash is one of the most powerful products in the Adobe Creative Suite family. With their frequent enhancements and developments, Adobe Flash has become a versatile multitasking application that allows you to create websites, desktop applications, mobile applications, cartoon animations, and more.

The secret behind Flash is that it has been developed side by side with the newest trends in web technology, such as the Rich Internet Applications. Another secret is the diverse capabilities within ActionScript, which have helped Flash extend its implementations into various projects, especially ActionScript 3 and other Object-Oriented Programming concepts.

Flash presents an innovative tool for both designers and developers in creating websites and developing interactive designs. Along with the expansion of Flash, Adobe also released a developer version called *Flex*, and later renamed it *Flash Builder*. This tool is directed toward code lovers who would like to build intensive code applications in both Flash and Flash Builder. At the same time, Adobe also released *Flash Catalyst* for designers like me, who do not like to write a single line of code.

Flash Catalyst is a platform for designers for creating interactive wireframes, websites, and user interfaces based on previous designs that they can import from other Adobe design tools like Photoshop and Illustrator.

In Flash Catalyst, the design elements can also be converted into interactive components, which will be explored in this book. However, Flash Catalyst is not a substitute for Flash Builder, as it does not take care of the whole coding process, but only creates the basic interactions that can be used in creating wireframes for projects and basic application interactions.

In this book we are going to discuss the different components of this software, and then briefly look at how Flash Catalyst can help us add interactivity to static designs.

After going through the workflow, we will learn how to export projects to either SWF for web use, or AIR-installable applications for desktops.

Let's start with a quick overview of the Flash Catalyst interface and the structure of its panels.

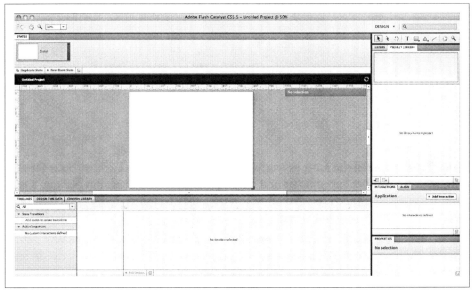

Figure 1-1. Flash Catalyst CS 5.5

Flash Catalyst is very simple in its design and looks similar to other Adobe tools. Its workspace includes the following panels and features:

- The *Pages/States* panel lets you add pages to your projects, components to pages, and states to the buttons.

- The *Breadcrumbs* bar shows where you are in the artwork. For example, when you enter a component you want to edit, it will appear as a path at the top right of the workspace. The Breadcrumbs bar enables you to easily move around the project or the stage area by simply clicking on the path.

- The *Tools* panel includes the basic shapes and tools you can create directly in Flash Catalyst.

- The *Layers* panel displays the layers of the imported files inside Flash Catalyst. You can also use it to create new layers when you want to create elements directly inside Catalyst.

- The *Library* panel includes the elements and *components* that you have created or imported into Flash Catalyst.

- The *Align* panel allows you to align objects with each other on the stage area.

- The *Interaction* panel helps you set the interaction properties for the components, such as the buttons.

- The *Properties* panel displays the properties of each object or component on the stage.
- The *Appearance* panel contains the blending modes and object properties.
- The *Filter* panel lets you add filters to the images and objects onto the stage.
- The *Timeline* panel is where you can add transitions between objects and pages.
- The *Common Library* contains a collection of wireframes and placeholders that can be used inside Flash Catalyst. These wireframes are either Flash Catalyst or Flex components, or just *placeholders*.
- The *Component HUD* is not a panel, but it becomes visible when you select a text or a component. You can use it to convert graphic elements into components, or to edit an existing component on the stage.

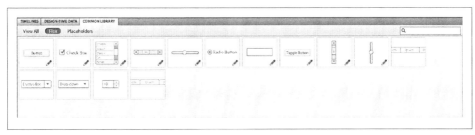

Figure 1-2. The new Common Library panel in Flash CS5.5

The above panels are parts of the Flash Catalyst *Design workspace*. If you would like to preview the code behind the project design, you can switch to the *Code Workspace* from the Window menu.

Figure 1-3. The Code Workspace in Flash Catalyst CS 5.5

The Code Workspace includes the code of the project in *MXML*. The Side Navigation panel allows you to navigate between project files, while the Problems panel at the bottom allows you to check the code errors.

CHAPTER 2

Flash Catalyst Components

As we mentioned before, Flash Catalyst uses components to build user interfaces and wireframes. In the new Flash Catalyst CS5.5, these components are found in the Common Library. In this chapter we will go through the components to understand their different types, and in the following chapters we will learn how to customize them.

In the Common Library panel, the components are classified into three categories:

- The *Flash Catalyst components* are editable components that can be customized and are able to interact with other content inside Flash Catalyst.
- *Flex components* are Flash Builder-based, therefore they are not functional in Flash Catalyst; you need to import your project into Flash Builder to be able to work with these components.
- *Placeholders* are objects that will be replaced by the actual objects in Flash Builder. They are used for marking the places of common objects, such as charts, avatars, maps, etc.

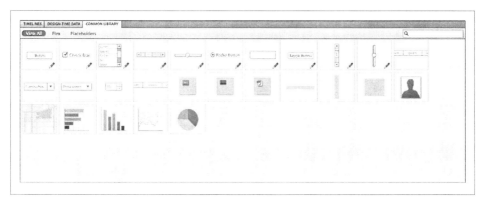

Figure 2-1. The available components in Flash Catalyst

Now, let's go through each component of Flash Catalyst and learn how to edit them.

Button

This component converts the artwork into an interactive button you can use to execute specific actions from the Interaction panel.

To add a button to the stage, just drag the *Button* component from the *Common Library* at the bottom of the workspace.

You can edit a button by double-clicking it to give it a customized name, or you can click on any of the button states in the *HUD*. When you activate the button-editing mode, you will notice that in addition to the *scale handles*, the component also contains the *constrain handles dots*. When you click on these constrains, a guide appears between the component edges and document edges to show the distance between the edges of the project and the component.

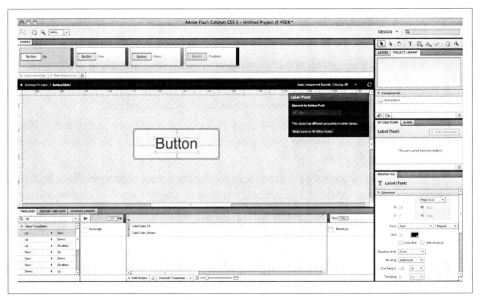

Figure 2-2. The Button component's different states

The *Button* component includes the following four options for button states:

- *Up* is the normal state of the button when no interaction is made.
- The *Over* state is when the user hovers over the button with the mouse.
- The *Down* state is when the user clicks on the button.
- The *Disabled* state shows when the button is inactive.

You can either use default shapes for the button states, or customize them with your own design.

Checkbox and Radio Button

These are components for forms. They are default shapes. They consist of two parts, the *checkbox* and the *label*, which is the one that includes the text.

The *Checkbox* includes the eight states listed below:

- *Up*
- *Over*
- *Down*
- *Disabled*
- *Selected, Up*
- *Selected, Over*
- *Selected, Down*
- *Selected, Disabled*

Figure 2-3. The Checkbox and Radio Button components

These states are similar to button states; the difference is that they only show the states in two cases: the selected and unselected.

Horizontal and Vertical Scrollbars

These two components are similar in structure and are used for creating scrolling content. When you drag any of them onto the stage and double-click to edit them, you will notice that they have three states: *Active*, *Inactive* and *Disabled*.

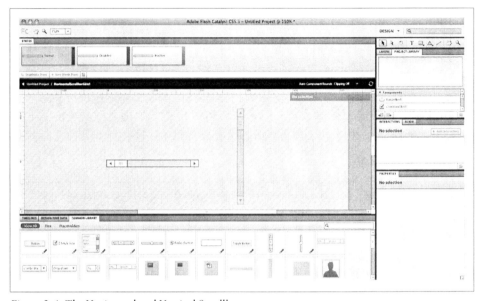

Figure 2-4. The Horizontal and Vertical Scrollbars

The artwork of the scrollbar consists of the following:

- The *Up* and *Down* buttons allow the user to scroll up and down. In the *Horizontal scrollbars*, the buttons represent the left and right buttons.
- The *Thumb* part is the scrolling part that the user can click and drag.
- The *Track* part is the background of the moving thumb that indicates the active area in which the thumb will move.

While you customize your own artwork and convert it into a scrollbar, some parts are essential for creating the components; these are the Thumb and the Track. If you had not defined the *Up* and *Down* buttons previously, you will get a scrollbar without up and down buttons.

Horizontal and Vertical Sliders

Unlike scrollbars, the *Slider* component does not include up and down buttons, but you can scroll the content by dragging the *Track* part.

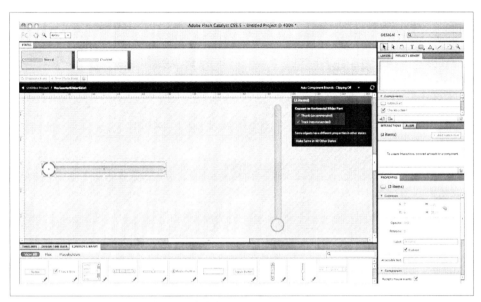

Figure 2-5. The Horizontal and Vertical Sliders

The *Horizontal* and *Vertical Sliders* consist of two main parts, the *Thumb* and the *Track*. The states for this component are either *Normal* or *Disabled*.

Text Input Component

This component is used for creating a text field where the user can enter specific information. When you enter the component-editing mode of the *Text Input* component, you will notice that it contains the input text field, which you can find in the *HUD* named as *Editable Text*.

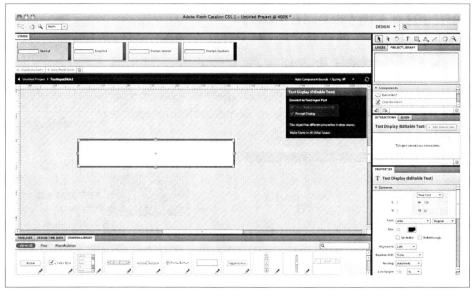

Figure 2-6. The input text component

You can edit the style and format of the text field through the *Appearance* panel.

This component includes four states: *Normal*, *Disabled*, *Prompt Normal*, and *Prompt Disabled*.

Toggle Button

The *Toggle* button component allows you to toggle between two modes for buttons, both of which have eight states, as listed below:

- *Up*
- *Over*
- *Down*
- *Disabled*
- *Selected, Up*
- *Selected, Over*
- *Selected, Down*
- *Selected, Disabled*

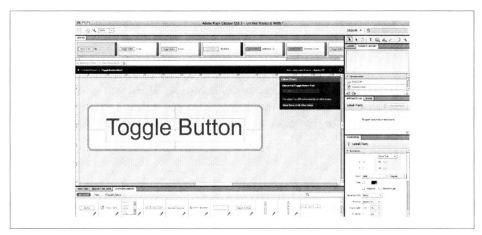

Figure 2-7. The Toggle button cases

These buttons consist of a required text label and an optional background image.

Data List Component

This component allows you to add multiple list items and scroll through them horizontally, or pan them vertically using horizontal and vertical scrollbars.

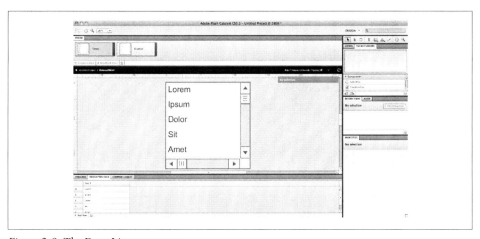

Figure 2-8. The Data List component

When you click to edit the component, you will notice that it contains the list content and both the vertical and horizontal scrollbars. These items are required for the component to work.

The repeated data list is a text area where you can add or edit list items through the *Design Time Data* panel at the bottom of the workspace. When you open this panel, you will notice that there are items listed in it. You can delete a value through the *Delete* icon at the bottom of the panel, or add new items with the Add Row button.

CHAPTER 3

Starting a Flash Catalyst Project

There are two methods by which you can start working with Flash Catalyst: you can either import artwork as *Photoshop PSD*, *Illustrator AI*, or *FXG* for *Adobe Fireworks*, or create the artwork in Flash Catalyst. Flash Catalyst's default components are only useful as wireframe tools, as they do not provide creative artwork, so if you are using Flash Catalyst to add interactivity to your creative design, it is preferable to create the artwork in Photoshop or Illustrator.

Figure 3-1. The New document dialog box

When you want to create a Flash Catalyst file from scratch, a dialog box appears for setting the file's dimensions and background color. But before you can create a Flash Catalyst file based on the imported Photoshop artwork, a dialog box appears where you can set the following:

- The Artboard size and color lets you set the file size and background color.
- The Fidelity section lets you choose from the following:
  — Keep the image layers editable or flatten its effects.

— Crop or flatten the shape layers.

— The text layer import options, such as editable text, vector outlines or flatten text layers.

• You can also choose whether you want to import the non-visible layers.

Figure 3-2. The Import PSD dialog box

You can also click the *Advanced* button to access the advanced dialog box where you can preview the layers of the artwork and each of their import options individually.

When you import an Illustrator artwork into Flash Catalyst, the import dialog box will look a little different, as Illustrator's import feature includes some extra options for converting or flattening blends and gradients. It also has an option for importing unused symbols.

Figure 3-3. The Import AI dialog box

In addition to importing *PSD*, *AI*, and *FXG* files, Flash Catalyst also allows you to import various types of other resources while you're working on the project, such as *SWF*, images, videos, and sound files. Images can be imported in *JPG*, *PNG*, *GIF*, and *JPEG* formats, videos in *FLV* or *F4V* formats, and sound files in *MP3* format.

In the example below, we will start by importing an Adobe Illustrator web page design into Flash Catalyst and then learn how to modify it in the Catalyst workspace.

1. Open Flash Catalyst and notice the *New from the Design File* part.
2. Choose *Create a New Project from Illustrator File* and open *webpage_ai.ai*.
3. In the import dialog box, make sure to keep all the elements editable so that you can modify them later.

Figure 3-4. Import Illustrator Artwork into Flash Catalyst project

This will import the web page design into the stage, and you will see that *Page1* is created in the *Page/Status* panel. The artwork layers and elements have also been imported into the Layers and Library panels.

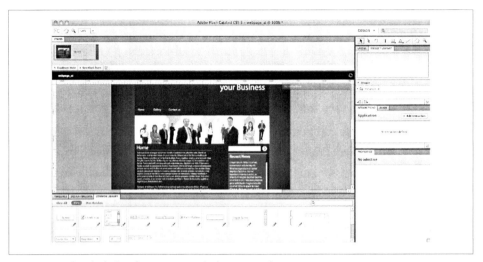

Figure 3-5. The Flash Catalyst project with the imported content

To start adding interactivity, first we need to convert the webpage elements into interactive components. Now, let us start converting the web design elements with the top menu and then continue by converting each link to a button component as follows:

4. Select the first link, *Home*, and from the *HUD*, choose to convert it to a button.

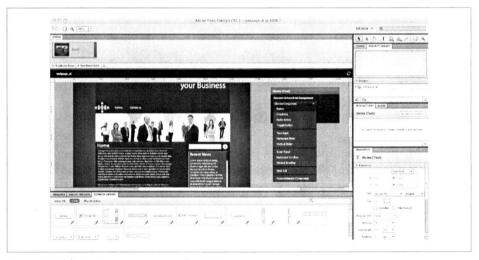

Figure 3-6. The Button component in the HUD

5. The text has been converted into a link, and the *HUD* now allows you to edit the button. Click on any of the button statuses to enter the *Button* editing mode.

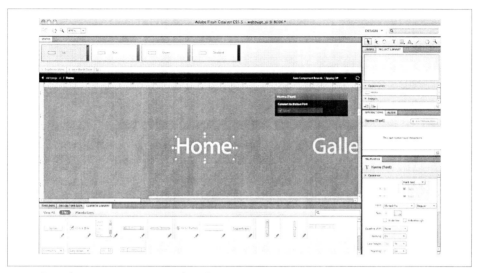

Figure 3-7. The Button component selected

6. Click the *Up* button in the *HUD*. You will find four statuses in the *Page/Status* panel. Keep the first status the same.

7. Select the *Over* status and draw a yellow rectangle under the text with the rectangle tool, as below. In the *Properties* panel, set the outline to none and the fill color to yellow.

Figure 3-8. The Over state of the button

8. In *Down* status, draw the same rectangle and change the opacity of the text to 50% in the *Properties* panel.

Figure 3-9. The Opacity value in the Properties panel

9. Repeat these steps with the rest of the menu links.

Now we will move on to the search white box to set the text input field as below:

10. Select the white area under the image.

11. From the *HUD*, select *Text Input* and click Edit.

Figure 3-10. The Text Input component in the HUD

12. Select the white box. Navigate to *Filter* in the *Properties* panel and choose *Inner Shadow*.

13. In the *Filter* properties, set the distance to *0* and the blur to *10*.

14. Deselect the white area and the text field above it. Now you can edit the input text properties, such as the font, size, color, etc.

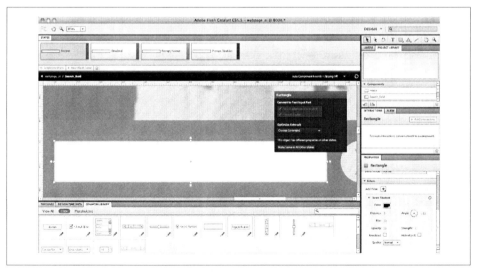

Figure 3-11. The search box background effect

15. Click the white area again to display the text field. You can choose to edit the text properties from the Properties panel. In this example, I just moved the text area to be aligned with the center of the white area.

16. After converting the white area into a text input field, we will need to convert the button next to it into clickable button, like we did with the menu above.

17. Select the button and from the *HUD*, choose the button component.

Figure 3-12. The search field button

18. Click the *Up* state in the *HUD* to enter the component editing mode. *Keep* the *Up* state with no change.

19. Activate the *Over* state, select the button, and change its opacity to 75% in the *Properties* panel.

Figure 3-13. The Over state button opacity

20. Active the *Down* state and choose the button artwork. Reduce the button size a little by dragging the scale box in the select area. You can also change its size in the Properties panel.

21. Now exit the button-editing mode by clicking on the root workspace on the *Breadcrumbs* bar.

22. Now test what we have done so far by choosing *File > Run Project*, or click `Cmd +Enter` (`Ctrl+Enter` in Windows).

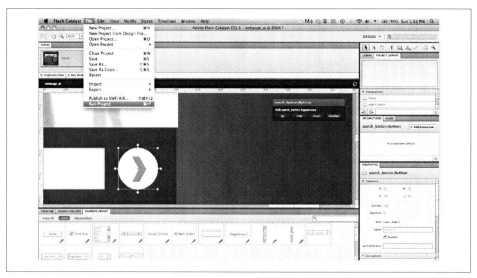

Figure 3-14. Run Project command.

After creating the search area, let us convert the scrolling text area under the search part into a functional component, as follows:

23. In the scrollbar area, select the gray scrolling background and the scrolling rectangle to convert it into a scrolling bar.

24. From the components *HUD*, select the *Vertical Scrollbar* and then click Edit to access the editing mode.

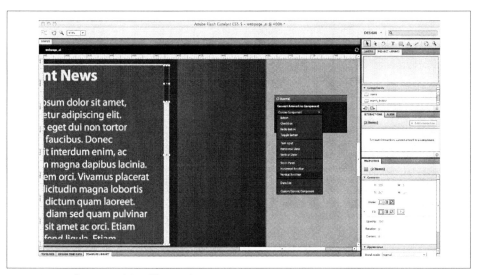

Figure 3-15. The Vertical Scrollbar in the HUD

25. Select the scrolling background and choose *Track* from the *HUD*. This background will act as the tracking area for the scrolling bar.

26. Select the top rectangle and choose *Thumb* from the *HUD*. This will be the scrolling part in the scrolling bar.

27. In some cases, the scrollbar may include the navigation top and bottom buttons. These buttons need to be defined as *Up* Button and *Down* Button in the component settings.

28. Go back to the root workspace and select both the text and the scrollbar components we have created.

29. You will notice that the rest of the text is hidden, which means that the text area does not display all the content.

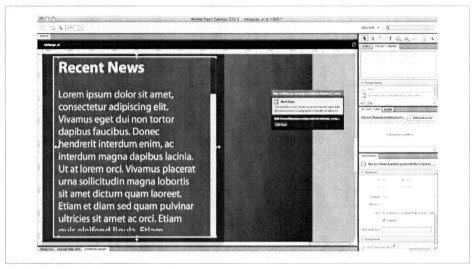

Figure 3-16. The scrolling text

30. From the *HUD*, choose the *Scroll Panel* to merge the scrollbar and the text associated with it.

31. Enter the component-editing mode and select the text. Choose *Scrolling Content* from the drop-down list of the *HUD*.

Figure 3-17. Converting the text field to scrolling content.

32. Click `Cmd+Enter` (`Ctrl+Enter` in Windows) to test the scrolling functionality and how the scrollbar scrolls to display the hidden text.

On the left side, the *Read More* link will point to an external URL. In the next steps, we will convert this text into a link to which we can add interaction later:

33. Select the Read More text and choose the *Button* component from the *HUD*.

34. Click the Up state in the *HUD* to enter the component-editing mode.

35. In the *Over* state, select the text and set its opacity to 75% in the *Properties* panel.

36. Using the *Rectangle* tool, draw a thin line under the text, which will appear when the user hovers over it.

37. Repeat the same steps in the *Down* state and exit the component-editing mode.

By this point, we have prepared the first page and converted the required areas into components for interaction. Before moving on to the interaction part, we will need to import the rest of the website pages that will be linked together through the top navigation menu.

In the second page, we will learn about adding videos to Flash Catalyst projects. Importing videos is as simple as importing other content like images, SWF, and sounds.

You can create a new page by clicking the New Blank State icon in the Page/State top panel and importing the new web design to it through the File→Import command, or you can click the Duplicate State icon to duplicate the current web design. In our example, we will duplicate the first page to get a similar page to the first one, and we will customize it as follows:

38. Click the Duplicate State icon in the *Page/State* panel and rename the second page *Gallery*.

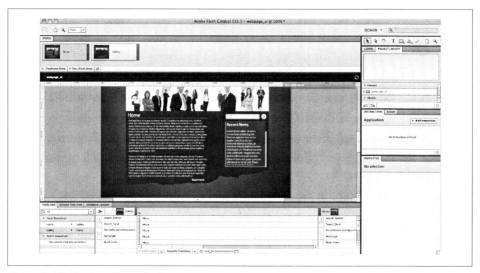

Figure 3-18. The Page/State duplicate content

39. Move the text content, the scrolling content, and the search area out of the stage and hide their layers in the *Layers* panel. Now you will have the content area empty and ready to import the video.

40. Select the header image and hide it from the Layers panel. After this, set the image under it as the header image for the page.

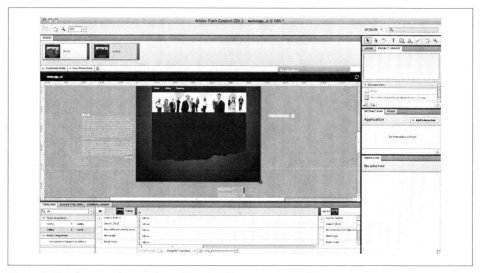

Figure 3-19. The second page after taking the 1ˢᵗ page content off screen

41. From the *File* menu, choose *Import→Video and Sound*

42. Navigate to FLV video *Video_sample.flv* and click import.

43. The video is now imported into the stage as a component, with the wireframe player associated with it.

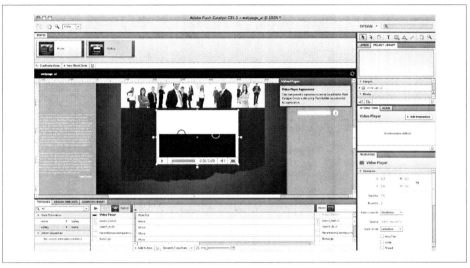

Figure 3-20. Import FLV video to the stage

In the *Properties* panel, the video properties include the following:

- The *Video controller* drop-down list, which lets you set the player's skin to either wireframe or standard, or allows you to remove the player from the video.

- The *Scale* mode lets the user set the scaling option when they click on the Full Screen icon on the player.

- You can also set the video to *autoplay*, *loop* when finished, and *mute* to play the video without sound.

- In the text section, you can change the text properties of the video controller, such as the size of the *time code* and the color of the video controller.

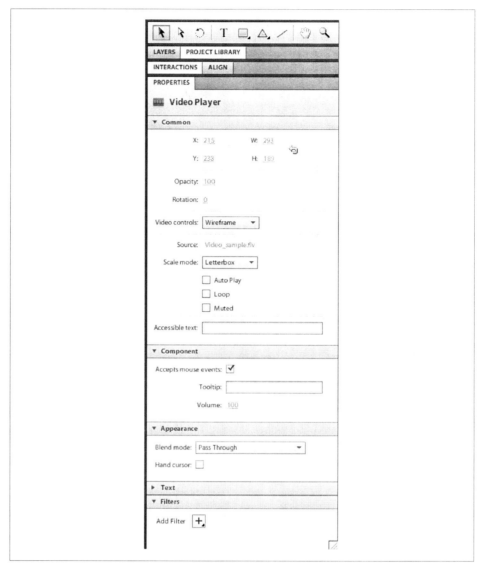

Figure 3-21. The video properties in the Properties panel

44. You can resize the video by dragging the video's edges to fit in the content area. If you want to maintain the same size proportion, press the Shift key while dragging the edges.

45. Test the current video properties by choosing *Run Project* in the File menu.

46. Since we will use our own *Play* and *Stop* custom buttons, we need to remove the current controller. In the video *Properties* panel, choose *None* from the Video Controls option.

Figure 3-22. Choose None from the controller drop-down list

47. Make the video buttons layer visible in the Layers panel in order for the video Play and Stop buttons to be displayed on the stage.
48. Place the buttons under the video.
49. Click the player button and form the *HUD*, choose the *Button* component, then click the Up state to enter the editing mode for this component.

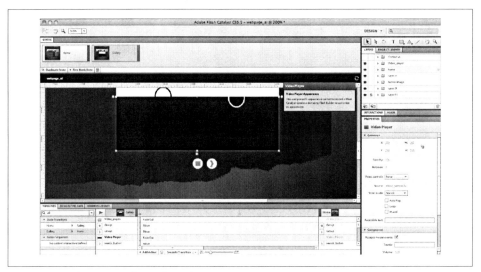

Figure 3-23. The custom play and stop buttons

50. The current state is 75% transparent. Now select the Over state and set the opacity of the button to 100%.

51. Repeat the above steps with the pause button.

As we mentioned above, in the current stage, we are setting up the artwork for interaction. In the next chapter we will learn how to add interaction to the components we have created, including the video controllers.

After completing the settings for the second page, we will add a new page to create the contact page as follows:

52. Click *Duplicate* State in the *Page/State* panel and take the video and the controllers' content off the design stage and hide them through the *Layers* panel. Rename the duplicated page *Contact us*.

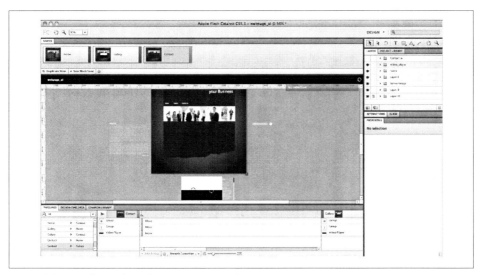

Figure 3-24. Duplicate the video page to create the contact page

53. Make the contact layer visible in the Layers panel to reveal the contact form fields.
54. Place the contact form fields in the content area.

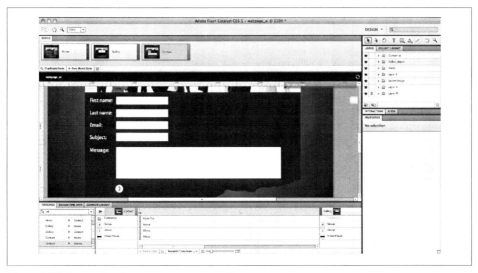

Figure 3-25. Importing the contact page artwork

55. Select the first white area and then go to the *HUD* to convert the selected area into a Text Input component.
56. Repeat this with the other form fields as well.

57. Select the form button and convert it into a button component.

By this stage, we have finished converting the web design artwork into an interactive component in Flash Catalyst. We will use these elements in the next chapter to interact with each other and link the pages together. For further interactivity and more complex Flash projects, you can export your project to Flash Builder and add more components and functions to it.

CHAPTER 4

Interactions and Transitions in Flash Catalyst

The purpose of converting the artwork into components was to prepare them for executing specific actions and transitions between pages, as we will discuss in this chapter.

I chose to cover both interactions and transitions in the same chapter because they are linked together, as transitions in Flash Catalyst are done through either opening a specific page or clicking a specific button. In this chapter we will start by looking at adding interaction to specific buttons, and after that we will move on to the interaction part.

Interaction in Flash Catalyst is done through the Interaction panel, which allows you to add actions either to the components similar to buttons, or the application itself. You can also add an action that is applied once the page is loaded, such as a special animation or a transition.

When you select a component or the applications stage by clicking on the stage area, the Add Interaction function will be activated.

The first drop-down list shows how the action will respond to the mouse action. For example, the On Click action indicates that the action will be executed when the user clicks on the component. The component interaction includes the following events that will trigger the action:

- *On Click*
- *On Double Click*
- *On Mouse Up*
- *On Mouse Down*
- *On Roll Out*
- *On Roll Over*

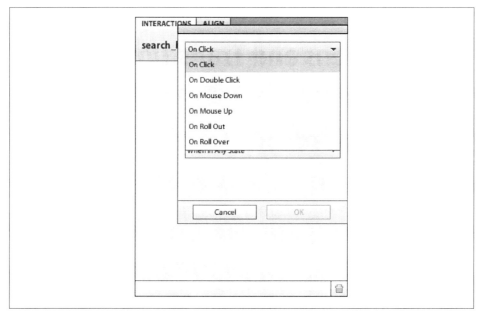

Figure 4-1. The components interaction event triggered

When you add an action to the application itself without any of the components selected, you will notice that the *On Application Start* is the only available option.

The Actions drop-down list includes the following actions:

- *Play Transition to State* is used for linking pages to each other by animated transitions between them, if applied.
- *Play Action Sequence* lets you play a specific set of actions in the timeline.
- The *Go to URL* opens a URL when the user clicks on it. You can also set how you want the new URL to be opened (for example, in a new page).
- *Play Video*
- *Pause Video*
- *Stop Video*

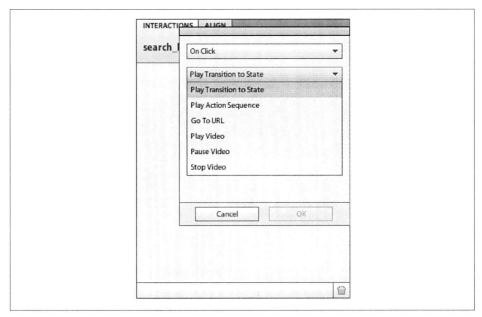

Figure 4-2. The Action drop-down list

Each of the actions has its own options, as we will see in the steps below.

In the previous steps, we saw that the project consists of three pages that are linked together by the top menu navigation. Here we will continue adding interaction to this menu so that we can navigate between pages. We will also add interaction to other parts of the design as follows:

1. If you did not rename the pages already, double-click the first page and name it *Home*. Repeat this with the second and third pages and name them Gallery and Contact us.

Figure 4-3. Renaming the Pages in the Page/State panel

2. Make sure you are on the first page. Select the first *Home* button.
3. Open the Interaction panel and click *Add Interaction*. From the action trigger, choose *On Click*.

Figure 4-4. Add Interaction to the button

4. From the Actions drop-down list, choose *Play Transition* to State and from the *Choose state*, select the *Home* page.

5. From the Appearance section of the Properties panel, choose Hand cursor to display the hand when the mouse hovers over it.

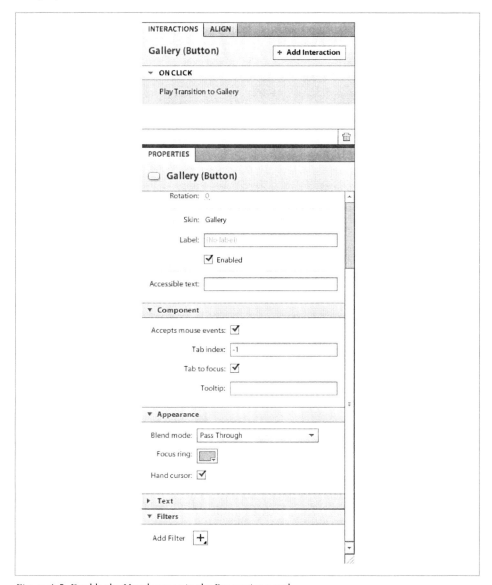

Figure 4-5. Enable the Hand cursor in the Properties panel

6. Repeat the above steps with the second and third button and link them to the *Gallery* and *Contact us* pages.

7. Move the *Read more* link under the text, then choose the *Go to URL* from the Actions drop-down list in the Interaction panel.

8. In the URL section, type the web address you would like to access, for example, www.oreilly.com (*http://www.oreilly.com*). You do not need to add HTTP://, because Flash Catalyst adds it by default.

Figure 4-6. Add Go to URL action to the button

9. From the next drop-list, choose Open in New Window to open the web page in a new browser window or tab.

10. Now let's move on to the second page. On this page, the *Gallery* button will not be active, and the first button—*Home*—will interact with the user to return to the first page. Select the *Home* button and from the Interaction panel, choose *Play Transition to State*, then select *Home* from the *Choose State* drop-down list.

11. In the Properties panel, choose the *Hand cursor* to display the hand.

12. Repeat this action with the *Contactus* button.

13. Repeat the same actions in the third page, *Contact us*.

14. Choose the play button of the video, and from the Interaction panel, choose *Play video* and then choose the video name from the drop-down list.

15. Select the video stop button and choose *Stop video* in the *Interaction* panel.

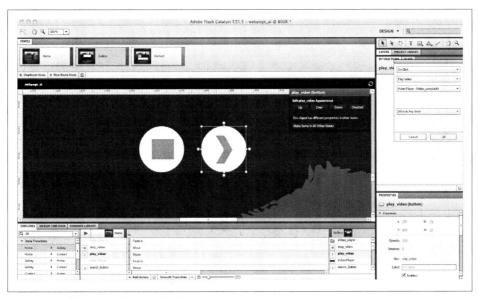

Figure 4-7. The play and stop video buttons

16. Test the project by pressing Cmd+Enter (Ctrl+Enter in Windows) to check the pages' navigation between each other.

These steps show an example of the interaction we can create in Flash Catalyst. Both the interactions and the transitions work closely together, since adding transitions and animations between pages and over buttons also improves the interactivity of the design, as we will see in the next part.

Before we discover how animations and transitions work in Flash Catalyst, let's discuss the Timeline panel. It is quite different from the timelines we have in Flash or After Effects, which depend on keyframes and in between frames.

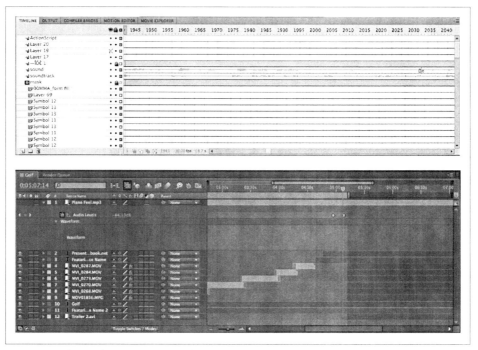

Figure 4-8. The timeline in Flash and After Effects

Unlike in those applications, transitions in the Flash Catalyst timeline are controlled by start points and end points. For example, if you want to create a fade in transition between two pages, you have to determine the first page where the animation starts from and the end page where the animation will end. The animation displays as a block in the timeline, as we can see in the figure about the anatomy of the timeline below.

Figure 4-9. The timeline in Flash Catalyst

- The *State Transitions* section includes all possible transition combinations between states and pages. Also, it contains the action sequences.

- The second section is the start page or state, which defines the start point of the animation. Below it you will find all the elements of the page in layers; each layer should display the animation associated with each element.

- The animation part shows the transition in a green block with a handle on its right, which controls the duration of the transition. By increasing the green area, you can make the animation slower, whereas if you decrease it, the animation will get faster. If more than one transition effect is associated with an object, you will find them under each other, linked to their layers. When you choose one of the transitions, you will notice that its properties appear in the properties panel where you can set its options, such as duration and easing.

- The end state is on the right side of the timeline and shows the end point of the animation, which can either be a page or a component state.

- The bottom section lets you create smooth transitions between the states and set their smoothness. You can add other types of transitions such as *Move*, *Resize*, *Rotate*, and *3D Rotate*. The *Zoom slider* lets you zoom in and out of the timeline blocks so that you can see more of the areas in the timeline. Also, you can delete any of the animations by selecting them and clicking the delete icon.

Figure 4-10. The Add Action list in the Timeline panel

Now we will learn how to add transition effects to our project by animating each element through the timeline.

First, we will need to play a transition when the page loads. Based on the idea we discussed before, the animation should have start and end points. We will need to create a new duplicated page from the first Home page, which we can add to the beginning of the page sequence.

In this page we will position the elements to the start point of the animation.

We will also need to tell Flash Catalyst that this newly created page is the default start page, as every project must have a default start page. You can easily find this default page through the dot in the page or state in the Page/State panel. Let's see how to apply this concept to our example as below:

17. Select the *Home* page in the *Page/State* panel and click *Duplicate State* to create a duplicated version of the home page.

18. Double-click on the duplicated version and name it *Start*.

19. Right-click the *Start* page and select Set as Default. This way, the animation will start with the *Start* page.

20. Click on the *Start* page stage without selecting any element. From the Interaction panel, choose *Play Transition to State* and choose target the *Home* page.

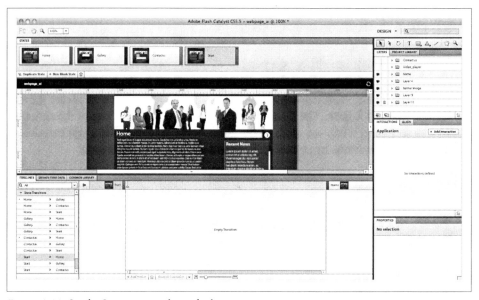

Figure 4-11. Set the Start page as the Default page

In the *Start* page, we are going to set the elements to the first position of the animation as follows:

21. In the Timeline panel, make sure you are selecting the *Start→Home* on the right side of the panel.

22. Drag the webpage logo to the top of the screen. You will notice that a green block appears on the timeline next to the logo layer to show that there has been a change in the logo position between the Start page and the Home page.

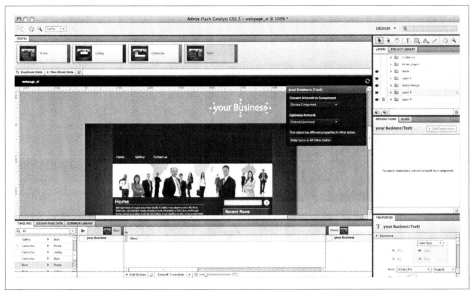

Figure 4-12. Animating the webpage logo

23. While the logo is still selected, click on the *Smooth transition* to create a smooth change in the animation's position.

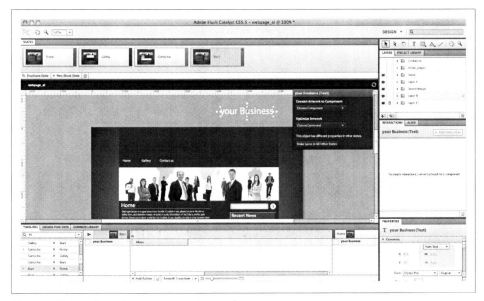

Figure 4-13. The Smooth animation in the timeline

24. Select each of the top menu buttons and set their opacity value to 0% in the Properties panel.

Figure 4-14. The top menu animation

25. Select the image and shrink it into thin line in the banner area, using the resize handlers in the transform rectangle. Then click *Smooth Transition* to create a smooth animation.

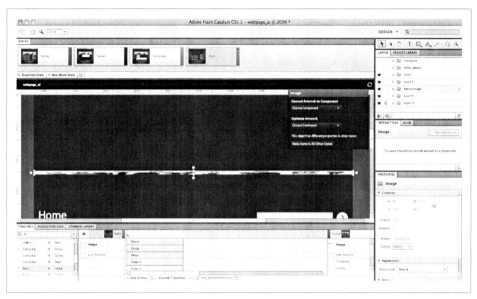

Figure 4-15. The banner image animation

26. Now select the Home page title, the line under it, the paragraph text, and the *Read more* button. Move all of them to the left of the screen stage and set their transition to smooth.

27. Select the search text area and the button next to it and set their opacity to 0%.

28. Drag the scrolling text content and background to the right side of the screen off the stage.

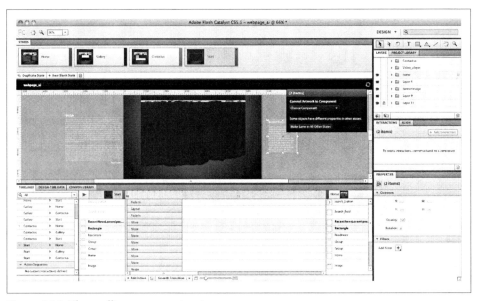

Figure 4-16. The scrolling content animation setup

29. If you want to preview the animation, click the *Play* button on the top right of the Timeline panel to preview the animation without having to run the project.

By this stage, we have created a transition that will appear when the user loads the project. However, the transition may not look the way you want it, as all the content is animated with the same timing and animation speed. It is a good idea to create some variations in the timing of each animation to make the transitions more interesting, as we will see in the following steps and the figure below:

30. Keep the transitions of the logo and the Home button the same.

31. Select the *Gallery* button and move it a little so that it will appear after the Home button animation.

32. Select and drag the *Contact us* button to start after the *Gallery* button transition starts.

33. Drag the image banner animation's handler to start where the timeline does and end by the *Contact us* button's transition.

34. Change the transition time of the Home title, the line under it, the text, and the Read more button so that they appear one by one with intersected animations between them.

35. Drag the animation of the search text area, its button, and the scrollbar to appear after the *Read more* button.

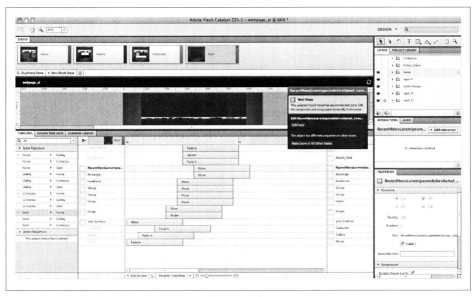

Figure 4-17. The timeline animation block after modifications

In addition to these, you can also improve the transitions by adding easing to the animations to give them a more realistic effect. The easing options are located in the Properties panel. But before we look at how to add the easing to the transitions, let's see the different easing types we can choose from:

- *Default* is when the animation moves at a constant rate from the beginning to the end of the transition.
- *Linear easing* starts slowly and keeps on its speed until the middle of the animation, then slows down again.
- *Sine* is a transition that moves fast until the middle of the animation and slows down toward the end.
- *Power* is similar to Sine, the only difference being that it includes an Exponent value that allows you to control the acceleration and deceleration of the transition.
- *Elastic* makes the transition swing before it reaches its end point.
- *Bounce* lets the transition move after the end point value and then return to the end point again.

Figure 4-18. The different easing options in the Properties panel

You can easily understand the difference between each easing if you look at how the curves appear under them to demonstrate how the transition will move. You can also edit the easing values through the properties related to each type.

Now, let's see how to apply easing methods to the transitions we have created previously.

36. Select the logo animation block. In the *Properties* panel, go to the *Easing* part and set the easing to *Bounce*.

37. Click the *Play* button to see how the easing will affect the animation's transition.

38. Select the *Home* title, the line under it, the paragraph, and the *Read more* part and set the easing to *Elastic*. Click the *Play* button to test the animation.

By this point, we have learned how to apply transition animations to the pages. In addition to the default transition properties, you can also add extra transitions by clicking the *Add Action* button next to the *Smooth Transition* button in the Timeline.

The Add Action button allows you to add the following actions:

- *Video Controls*, such as Play, Pause, and Stop.
- *SWF controls* that include Play SWF, Stop SWF, Go to Frame and Play, and Go to Frame and Stop.
- *Set Component State*
- *Set Property*, which lets you set a specific property for the component.

- *Fade*, which gives you the option to create a fade for the object from one state to another; you can set this in the Properties panel.
- *Sound Effects* lets you add a sound effect to the stage transition or component status, such as buttons.
- *Move*
- *Resize*
- *Rotate 3D* lets you create 3D transitions in the 3D space, such as rotating the object in the 3D axes values that are listed in the Properties panel.

Notice that the added transition properties are added as green animation blocks under the default one in the artwork layer in the timeline.

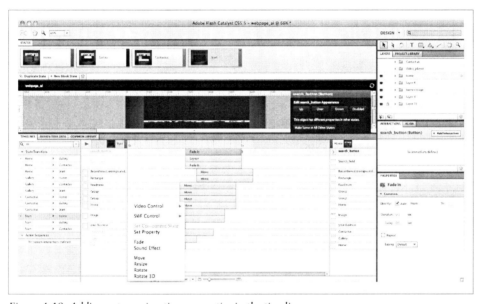

Figure 4-19. Adding extra animation properties in the timeline

These transition effects can be applied to the button statuses as well, so you can create animations that occur when the user hovers over a button, as we will see in the top menu button states.

In these buttons, we need to apply transitions for the lines under the menu text to appear along with a sound effect when the user hovers over it, as follows:

39. Double-click the Home button in the top menu to access the button editing-mode.

40. Move the rectangle under the text to the Up state a little below the text, and set its opacity to 0%.

Figure 4-20. The rectangle in the Up state

41. In the *Over* state, move the rectangle just under the text and set its opacity to 100%.

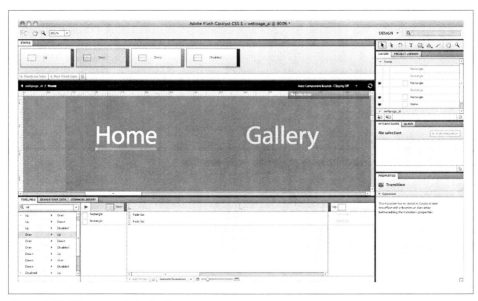

Figure 4-21. The rectangle in the Over state

42. Repeat what you did in the Up state in the Down state.

43. In the Timeline panel, select the *Up→Over* from the side list to change the animation between those two cases.

44. Select the rectangle's layer and choose Smooth Transition to create a smooth move when the user hovers over the button.

Figure 4-22. The button timeline smooth transition

45. In the *Up→Over* state we need to add a sound effect that will be played when the user hovers over the button. While the rectangle layer is selected, click *Add Action* and choose Sound Effect from the list.

Figure 4-23. Add Sound Effect from the Add Action list

46. A dialog box appears to let you select the sound effect from the available assets. Click the Import button to import sound effects.

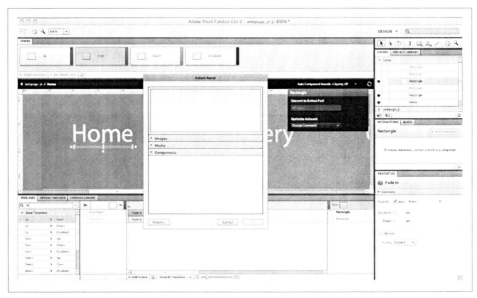

Figure 4-24. The Sound Effect dialog box

47. You can choose a sound effect from your own library or go to the Adobe Flash Catalyst sound effects folder (*Applications→Adobe Flash Catalyst CS5.5→Sound Effects* on a Mac, or *Program files→Adobe→Adobe Flash Catalyst CS5.5→Sound Effects* in Windows).

48. Select a sound file, for example *Electronic Slide.mp3*, and click OK.

49. You will find the sound files listed under the *Media* section. Choose one and click OK.

Figure 4-25. The selected sound listed in the Media section in the dialog box

50. Repeat the same rectangle animation actions with the *Over→Down* state to make the rectangle fade when the user clicks the button.

51. Press the *Play* button to test the button animation sequence.

In the above steps, we learned to create transitions between two pages that have the same content. Now let's see how to create transitions between two pages with different content.

When making a transition between two pages with different content, the content of each page should be located in both pages. This way, you can control the fade in and fade out of the content during the transition, as we will see on the Home and Gallery pages below.

52. Select the *Home→Gallery* from the state transition side list in the Timeline. You will notice that the *Gallery's* page content is put outside the screen in the *Home* page. On the other hand, the Home page's content is still located in the *Gallery* page outside the workspace.

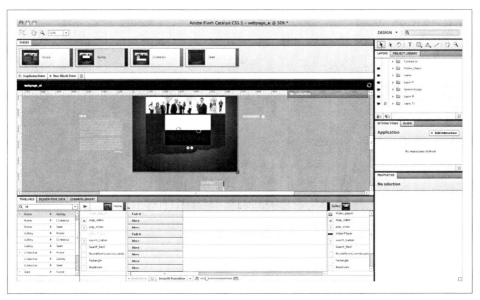

Figure 4-26. The Home→Gallery stage animation

53. Select all the elements in the Home page and click Smooth Transition to create an animated move off screen for the Home elements. Then move the animation to its position in the stage for the Gallery elements.

54. You can edit the transitions and apply easing options as we did in the previous steps.

In this chapter, we have learned to add interactivity and animated transitions to our project.

Now let's see how to create user interfaces or web pages in Flash Catalyst based on imported artworks from Adobe Illustrator, and how to convert the artworks into functional components.

After finishing the project or wireframe and testing it, the project can be published in either *SWF* or *AIR* formats, as we will see in the next chapter.

CHAPTER 5

Publishing the Flash Catalyst Project

This is the final step in the design or wireframe project process, in which we are going to learn how to publish projects in SWF format to display them on the web, or in AIR format to create desktop-installable applications.

As we saw in the previous example, we do not need to publish the project to see it while we are still working, but it is possible to preview it through File→Run Project, or by pressing Cmd+Enter (Ctrl+Enter in Windows) to run the project in the default browser.

You can publish the project by choosing *Publish SWF/AIR* from the File menu or using the shortcut Shift+Cmd+F12 (Shift+Ctrl+F12 in Windows).

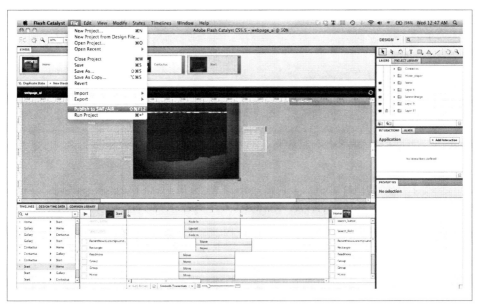

Figure 5-1. Publish SWF/AIR from the File menu

Since Flash Catalyst does not provide extensive functionality, many users export their Flash Catalyst projects to Flash Builder to complete them. However, it is preferable to do the publish step in Flash Builder rather than Catalyst.

The Publish *SWF/AIR* dialog box in Flash Catalyst includes the following options:

- The Output directory is the location where the published project will be saved.
- Build for Accessibility checkbox
- Build version for uploading to web server checkbox
- Build version to view offline checkbox
- Build AIR application checkbox
- Embed fonts

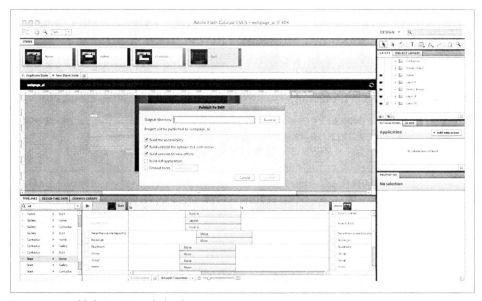

Figure 5-2. Publish SWF/AIR dialog box

The *Embed fonts* option allows you to embed fonts in Flash Catalyst projects. If the project does not include any fonts to embed, this option will not be selectable.

The advantage of embedding the font in the project is that you can make sure that the user will see the project as you designed it, even if they do not have the font installed on their computer. Make sure to only embed the fonts that will not be available on the user's computer, otherwise this will affect the size and performance of your project.

When you click publish, you will notice that Flash Catalyst saves three versions of the project to the specified location: a web version, a local version, and an AIR application version. The web version includes the *SWF*, the *HTML* container, the *SWFObject.js*, and the files that will ensure that the application runs properly on your client's computer.

Project Performance

Running an optimized project can help the application load faster and prevents the computer from consuming a lot of the CPU resources. However, it is important to consider the following optimization tips to help you create fast-loading applications.

Remove the unnecessary artwork or components from the project at each state. For example, if you have an element that is not used in the state and is not part of the state transition, you can delete this element by selecting it and clicking the Delete key. Note that the element may appear nonfunctional in a specific state but can still be part of the transition animation. If you remove it from this state, the transition will not work properly.

The second tip is optimizing the artwork through the Optimize Artwork drop-down menu from the *HUD*. In this menu, you have different optimization options, such as:

Optimize Vector Graphics
> This option allows you to compress the vector elements in the design. If you choose it, you will notice that the HUD displays Optimized Graphics in the element title.

Rasterize
> In some cases, the complex vector graphics can cause huge CPU consumption, which may result in slow performance, even if the size of the project is fine. In this case, converting the vector graphics into rasterized bitmaps will ensure that the project runs properly.

Compress
> This option allows you to compress the image by a specified percentage. Please note that the higher the compression percentage, the lower quality you get.

Convert to Linked Image
> This smart solution takes the image out of the project and loads it externally from the project folder. This option can decrease the project size and allows you easily edit images by replacing them in the external folder.

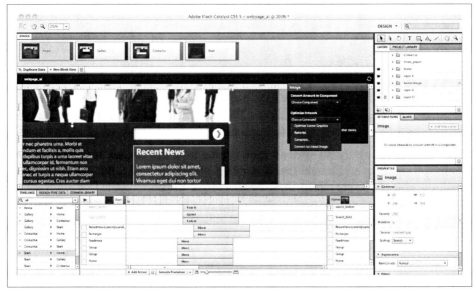

Figure 5-3. Optimize artwork options in the HUD

In this quick guide to Flash Catalyst CS5.5, we have learned how to import artwork, convert it into interactive components that can do specific actions, and how to apply animated transitions between project pages. Most of the other tasks in Flash Catalyst are based on these concepts and workflow, so you can start creating your own project and practice using the different options to create interactive UI or application wireframes.

You can learn more about Flash Catalyst CS5.5 through this Adobe link:

http://www.adobe.com/products/flashcatalyst.html

And you can find more learning resources in the following links:

http://tv.adobe.com/
http://www.adobe.com/devnet/flashcatalyst.html

About the Author

Rafiq Elmansy has been a graphic designer for 10 years and has a background in traditional art and sculpture. His graphic design experience includes working on different design projects as well as creative directing. He runs his own design company, Pixel Consultations (*www.pixelconsultations.com*). He is also an Adobe Community Professional, Adobe Certified Expert in Flash and Photoshop, and the founder and manager of the Adobe user group in Egypt (AUGE), the first Adobe user group in the Middle East. Rafiq is also part of the Adobe Prerelease Program and an author in the graphic and design field. His articles are published in the Adobe Design and Developer center, Adobe Edge, *communitymx.com*, and his design blog (*www.graphicmania.net*). He is the author of *Photoshop 3D for Animators* (Focal Press).

Colophon

The animal on the cover of *Quick Guide to Flash Catalyst* is a Nilotic Moniter.

The cover image is from *Riverside Natural History*. The cover font is Adobe ITC Garamond. The text font is Linotype Birka; the heading font is Adobe Myriad Condensed; and the code font is LucasFont's TheSansMonoCondensed.

Get even more for your money.

Join the O'Reilly Community, and register the O'Reilly books you own. It's free, and you'll get:

- $4.99 ebook upgrade offer
- 40% upgrade offer on O'Reilly print books
- Membership discounts on books and events
- Free lifetime updates to ebooks and videos
- Multiple ebook formats, DRM FREE
- Participation in the O'Reilly community
- Newsletters
- Account management
- 100% Satisfaction Guarantee

Signing up is easy:

1. **Go to: oreilly.com/go/register**
2. **Create an O'Reilly login.**
3. **Provide your address.**
4. **Register your books.**

Note: English-language books only

To order books online:

oreilly.com/store

For questions about products or an order:

orders@oreilly.com

To sign up to get topic-specific email announcements and/or news about upcoming books, conferences, special offers, and new technologies:

elists@oreilly.com

For technical questions about book content:

booktech@oreilly.com

To submit new book proposals to our editors:

proposals@oreilly.com

O'Reilly books are available in multiple DRM-free ebook formats. For more information:

oreilly.com/ebooks

O'REILLY®

Spreading the knowledge of innovators   oreilly.com

The information you need, when and where you need it.

With Safari Books Online, you can:

Access the contents of thousands of technology and business books

- Quickly search over 7000 books and certification guides
- Download whole books or chapters in PDF format, at no extra cost, to print or read on the go
- Copy and paste code
- Save up to 35% on O'Reilly print books
- **New!** Access mobile-friendly books directly from cell phones and mobile devices

Stay up-to-date on emerging topics before the books are published

- Get on-demand access to evolving manuscripts.
- Interact directly with authors of upcoming books

Explore thousands of hours of video on technology and design topics

- Learn from expert video tutorials
- Watch and replay recorded conference sessions

Spreading the knowledge of innovators   safari.oreilly.com

Lightning Source UK Ltd.
Milton Keynes UK
UKOW021025141112

202166UK00003B/20/P